PROMOTOR, SUPPRESSOR, OR NEUTRALIZER

Impact of Latest AI and Geopolitics on Global Outsourcing

Stephan S. Sunn

Davidson Global Partners, LLC

Copyright © 2024 Stephan S. Sunn

©Copyright 2024 -2026 Stephan Sun All Rights Reserved

Disclaimer:

This book may not be reproduced or transmitted in any form without the written permission of the authors. Every effort has been made to make this guide as complete and accurate as possible. Although the authors have prepared this guide with the greatest of care, and have made every effort to ensure its accuracy, we assume no responsibility or liability for errors, inaccuracies, or omissions. Before you begin, check with the appropriate authorities to ensure compliance with all laws and regulations. Every effort has been made to make this report as complete and accurate as possible. However, there may be mistakes in typography or content. Also, this report contains information on online marketing and technology only up to the publishing date. Therefore, this report should be used as a guide – not as the ultimate source of Internet marketing information. The purpose of this report is to educate. The authors do not warrant that the information contained in this report is fully complete and shall not be responsible for any errors or omissions. The authors shall have neither liability nor responsibility to any person or entity concerning any loss or damage caused or alleged to be caused directly or indirectly by this report, nor do we make any claims or promises of our ability to generate income by using any of this information.

Davidsons Global Associates & Co. LLC, Davidson, NC 28036, USA;   All Inquiries of copyrights, and cooperation go to: Stephan.sunn@aya.yale.edu

CONTENTS

Title Page
Copyright
Preface
Chapter 1: Outsourcing in the Age of AI and Geopolitics
Chapter 2: Strategic Implications of AI on Outsourcing
Chapter 3: Geopolitical Factors Affecting Outsourcing
Chapter 4: Evolving Business Models in Outsourcing
Chapter 5: Redefining Workforce Management
Chapter 6: New Client Relationships and Delivery
Chapter 7: AI-Enabled Competitive Advantages
Chapter 8: The Enduring Value of People in the AI Era
Chapter 9: Future Trends and Recommendations
Acknowledgement
About The Author
Books By This Author

PREFACE

The author and his partners contributing to this series of professional guidance and industry best practices possess over two decades of experience advising multinational corporations and C-suite executives. They are esteemed thought leaders within their respective fields and globally renowned throughout their extensive professional networks. Prior to the COVID-19 pandemic, when international travel was unencumbered, they would convene annually at a rotating global location. Their first reunion following that worldwide crisis was imbued with a profound sense of gratitude for having endured such a cataclysmic event.

Reuniting with one another brought joy to all of us. Even more so, the notion of how delicate and short life began to settle in. The idea of documenting our business experience and lessons, successes or failures, to help our colleagues and clients was formed in 2022 when we gathered in Jamaica. However, with the arrival of ChatGPT and similar trailblazing AI technologies in late 2022, this small proposal gains urgency because we fear within the next decade these revolutionary technologies could transform our lives and society forever, and resemble what COVID-19 has brought to us.

The subject matter of this book series are the business domains we have supported clients worldwide last two decades, with the priority in the last few years. We don't claim we are the researchers or professors in the technologies, but the practitioners who evaluate, choose, and apply state-of-the-art technologies to solve business problems. The technology breakthroughs are not what we pursued, the critical criterion is if the technology solved the business problems with business values. This is why "Case Studies", "Examples" or "Lessons" are weighted much higher than the rigorous analytics of the theories in these business guides.

This book explores how artificial intelligence (AI) and geopolitics are transforming the global outsourcing industry. It analyzes the strategic implications of AI for outsourcing operations, delivery models, talent management, and client relationships. The impact of geopolitical forces like trade tensions, political instability, and regulatory shifts on risk mitigation and geographic diversification is examined.

Emerging business models combining AI and human expertise, niche services, innovation through collaboration, workforce upskilling, and ethical AI governance are highlighted. The book provides a strategic roadmap for international outsourcing providers to navigate challenges, seize opportunities, and drive sustainable growth in this era of technological disruption and evolving geopolitical dynamics.

CHAPTER 1: OUTSOURCING IN THE AGE OF AI AND GEOPOLITICS

Since its inception, the global outsourcing industry has made an incredible journey from being a pure cost-cutting tool to becoming an increasingly intricate and multidimensional business model that leverages global talent, resources, and expertise. As we enter a new era driven by rapid advancements in artificial intelligence (AI) and an increasingly turbulent geo-political landscape, cross-border vendors are venturing into uncharted territories to differentiate and grow in a sustainable way.

The outsourcing journey is traditionally fueled by the relentless focus and drive to cut costs, enhance operational efficiencies, and concentrate on core competencies. This has been primarily achieved through labor arbitrage by offshoring non-core functions to low-cost locations like India, China, and the Philippines. However, as an industry matures, the focus has significantly shifted to value creation, innovation and strategic partnerships.

AI has become the catalyst that remarkably alters the canvas of outsourcing today. The promises it offers are reshaping how services are being delivered through a different level of automation efficiency, scalability, and accuracy from robotic process automation (RPA) to machine learning and natural language processing. Global vendors can fully tap AI's strengths in automating repetitive tasks, enhancing decision-making, and even providing more personalized services to customers.

However, the rise of AI is not without its difficulties, particularly in the field of offshoring. It is often argued that AI-enabled automation endangers human workers in some ways by displacing them. Additionally, there are moral and societal worries at stake in an increasingly viral world where prudence demands data protection—and in outsourcing partners' search for a useful, productive offshored work site, in the potentially vicious biases that AI algorithms can perpetuate.

Geopolitics contributes to the geography of the outsourcing business too. International trade treaties, border tariffs, and regional conflict—all shape the currents and eddies of outsourcing services, determining where an international seller can and can't serve clients. Take today, for instance. For a lot of outsourcing companies, the rising tide of trade tensions between the United States and China is cause to bite one's nails. As a result, some are diversifying geographically, and others taking entirely new consumer markets.

In addition, political instability, economic sanctions, and ever-shifting regulatory environments pose significant hazards to both transaction parties. The COVID-19 pandemic is just the newest sudden lesson that firms must be resilient and versatile in a world prone to sporadic international upsets. Suppliers must build strong risk mitigation plans and emergency operations schemes to preserve functionality whenever the next geopolitical skittle cascades.

Still, a backlash against outsourcing is unaffordable for the global economy. It is all too reliant on inexpensive foreign labor. India is the world's back office. It crunches the numbers. It writes the code. It does the math. It fields your phone call. It's where Xerox sends your phone complaint and GE ships your plane order.

Alone U.S. companies have 2 million Indians doing their tiniest bidding. Outsourcers in India do about $17B worth of business a year, a sum expected to quadruple by 2008, according to the National Association of Software and Service Companies, their trade association. And China? It's grabbing more and more of the goods part of the outsourcing equation. "Apple is outsourcing enough in China that America is stopping growing," says Nipun Mehta, president of software maker TBI Technologies.

Take into account the expenses of operating an Indian payroll. A programmer in New York City taunts his counterpart in Bangalore: "For $20,000," he says, "I'll do your job. I'll do it half as well and twice as slowly!" Well, yes. The typical American programming peon gets $60,000 in base pay, plus $12,000 in health and retirement benefits. He faces more taxes and lawsuits than his Indian confrere does. But the American toils more than 1,600 hours a year; she has 18 vacation days and maybe 10 sick days.

A software developer in India makes about $6000, and she receives benefits worth $1000. And she might work 2300 hours per year. Physicians in India man the front porch swing in the waiting room. Ambitious newlywed husbands work twenty-hour days. A median white-collar worker there "works" about fifty hours a week. Let's say that our California I.T. guy "only" works sixty hours per week.

Outsourcing's history tells us that it moved slowly from pure labor arbitrage to more strategic-value basis approaches. In the beginning, the drive to offshore was simply based on the desire to reduce costs. Companies started to send low-skill, labor-intensive jobs to places that had lower wages.

However, as the trade marketplace proliferated and diversified, many outsourcing firms started offering services that were considerably more advanced than simple manufacturing and assembly. Now, they offer software development, data analytics, and customer support. And as vendors' capabilities expanded, some started offering higher-value professional services as well: architecture, engineering, creative design, and legal services.

Three forces are responsible for this expanded range of leading services: business's inexorable globalization; the ongoing, rapid pace of technology change, which requires advanced skills and continual learning; and the rising need for companies to tap into specialized expertise and talent.

Right now, services outsourcing seems poised at a major inflection point, driven by advances in artificial intelligence and shifts in geopolitics. AI technologies are rapidly making it feasible for service providers to automate on a massive scale. From data entry to high-level decision-making, services outsourcing's calls and clicks increasingly are being answered by machines that can think. This AI-driven automation stands to deliver enormous savings, improve both the precision and the speed of service, and enable increasingly rich offerings.

A notable industry trend is the fusion of human expertise with AI capabilities, resulting in hybrid outsourcing models. Service providers are benefiting from this concept as it allows them to optimize their processes, cut expenses, and boost service quality. An example is that customer inquiries are handled through AI-powered chatbots while human agents process complex interactions. This interdependence between human intelligence and machine efficiency is reshaping conventional outsourcing and opening doors to innovation.

The Growing Sway of Custom Services With a more refined outsourcing market, the demand for tailored services equipped to deal with a specific industry vertical or a business function is enlarging. The popularity of bespoke services, i.e., financial crime detection, healthcare analytics, or supply chain optimization, is growing as businesses strive for ready-made solutions to unique complications.

There are also potentially significant risks in political instability and regional conflicts, especially in jurisdictions where institutions and governance structures are comparatively weak. The importance of resilience and adaptability through global disruptions is a key lesson of the COVID-19 pandemic. The providers have had to adapt rapidly to new working arrangements and to ensure business continuity.

We're going to explore in much more depth what AI and geopolitics really mean for the outsourcing industry in the strategy chapters that follow. We're going to go much further into the various kinds of challenges that are faced by international vendors and some of the opportunities.

With the help of case studies, expert insights from people who have lived through the onslaught of AI and geopolitics, and learning points, we aim to give you as close to a roadmap as we can get through the complexity of outsourcing in the AI and geopolitics era so that people can build enough resilience that they can drive the innovation they need and they can achieve sustainable growth.

CHAPTER 2: STRATEGIC IMPLICATIONS OF AI ON OUTSOURCING

The adoption of artificial intelligence (AI) is opening up a new set of possibilities for the outsourcing industry. As global service providers struggle with obstacles and opportunities presented by this dislocating technology, it becomes imperative to appreciate the strategic implications of AI for outsourcing operations and delivery.

One of the biggest advantages AI holds for the future of outsourcing is its capacity to boost efficiency, accuracy, and scalability to unprecedented levels. By taking over repetitive and time-consuming tasks, AI-powered capabilities can make companies located anywhere in the world more efficient, and reduce their costs and turnaround times. Robotic process automation (RPA) can for example be used for automating routine data entry, invoice processing, and customer support so that human staff can be deployed attending to more intricate and higher value-adding activities.

Additionally, analytics driven by AI can allow global vendors to process massive amounts of data swiftly and precisely, revealing deep insights into client behavior, market developments, and operational performance. This helps vendors make evidence-based choices, optimize their service ranges, and spot new growth and innovation prospects.

Another major benefit of having AI in offshoring is its ability to enhance the quality of service. By having machine learning algorithms and using natural language processing technologies, global vendors have come up with intelligent systems that are capable of understanding client queries better and providing a more accurate and faster response. As a result, customer satisfaction rises due to better vendor service delivery, reduced error rates, and increased client loyalty.

But there are also big challenges and ethical considerations in deploying AI in outsourcing. Job displacement is one of the primary concerns. Automation powered by AI threatens to eliminate many jobs currently performed by humans. This could have major social and economic implications, especially in developing countries where outsourcing has been a leading source of jobs and economic growth.

International vendors need to mitigate these risks through the creation of AI strategies that consider and prioritize the well-being of their workforce. This includes implementing reskilling and upskilling programs that help workers adapt to new roles and technologies, and developing ethical guidelines and governance frameworks that guarantee AI is being implemented fairly and transparently.

Another significant problem is the matter of data privacy and security. AI systems rely extensively on the accumulation and interpretation of massive amounts of information. That is why overseas developers have to guarantee the confidential materials of their customers with sturdy data protection control to obey with apposite regulations such as the European Union's GDPR.

Despite the above challenges, there are numerous examples of successful international vendor AI deployments across various sectors. For example, an Indian IT services company called Tata Consultancy Services (TCS) has created a platform named 'Ignio' that deploys AI to automate and streamline IT operations for its clients. Leveraging machine learning and cognitive automation, Ignio can predict and pre-empt system failures, reduce downtime, and improve overall efficiency.

Wipro, another prominent Indian IT services provider, has introduced a platform called "Holmes" that employs AI to systematize a broad array of business processes — from customer service to procurement. Through the marriage of RPA, machine learning, and cognitive computing technologies, Holmes has yielded substantial cost reductions and efficiency gains for Wipro's clients.

In the era of artificial intelligence (AI), the ever-changing outsourcing industry requires global providers to play a proactive, strategic role in embracing technology. This encompasses partnering with AI providers, committing to research and development (R&D) investments, and inculcating innovation and learning into their organizational culture.

Furthermore, global suppliers must also take into account the wider social and ethical consequences of AI adoption, and strive to ensure that the advantages of this game-changing technology are shared fairly among various stakeholders. This could mean partnering with governments, educational institutions, and non-governmental organizations (NGOs) to create responsible and inclusive AI regulations and methods.

To sum up, the strategic implications of AI on outsourcing are deep and wide. AI-driven solutions are capable of tremendous efficiency, accuracy and scalability. Nonetheless, they come with huge challenges and ethical concerns that need to be addressed systematically. In the age of AI-powered outsourcing, international vendors need to develop responsible and inclusive AI strategies, invest in talent and partnerships and build a culture of innovation and continuous learning.

CHAPTER 3: GEOPOLITICAL FACTORS AFFECTING OUTSOURCING

As the global economy continues to become more interconnected, the potential impact of geopolitical events on the outsourcing industry becomes increasingly pronounced. Barriers to trade, social turbulence, economic pullbacks, and changes in regional power relationships all contribute to a volatile landscape where multinational providers must operate to achieve operational equilibrium and manage risk. This chapter explores the leading geopolitical forces that shape outsourcing decisions and presents practical guidelines for assessing and managing risk effectively.

The geopolitical snowball's cascade ripples across supply chain management in a multitude of ways. Open trade wars, for instance, centered on today's geopolitical animosities between the United States and China, spawn tariff mania, convulse supply networks, and reorient market rivalries. In turn, these stimulations conspire to reconfigure provider cost structures, reanimate supplier audits qualify alternate sourcing, and trigger rolling adjustments in market entry planning.

In the places outsourcing suppliers do their work, political instability may put them at risk of not having the data safety, business continuity, and worker protection they require. Those suppliers have to be prepared to change and react to new government rules, social problems, and threats to safety. Those suppliers also have to adjust if sanctions against a nation reduce markets or sources, because of competition or future supply requirements.

Overview of a trade war and its impacts – The US-China trade war has had cascading consequences in the outsourcing industry. Higher tariffs and technological transfer restrictions have led certain US companies to reconsider outsourcing relationships with Chinese vendors. Other countries' players (e.g., India, Vietnam, Philippines) who can provide competitive pricing and niche services have found an avenue to reach customers through it.

Similarly, vendors operating in the global market now face greater uncertainty in their long-term planning due to the ambiguity surrounding the trade war. Tariffs, regulations, and also geopolitical tensions are ever-changing and force vendors to adopt a level of strategic agility and nimbleness. In response, vendors have been spreading themselves more broadly geographically and also among the industries they serve and also building distinguishing capabilities.

In order to navigate the intricate geopolitical landscape successfully, international outsourcing vendors must adopt diversification as a central strategy for mitigating risk. By spreading their geographic footprint across a variety of countries and regions, vendors can decrease their exposure to any one market and thus minimize the risk of localized disruptions.

Equally important is the broadening of service offerings. By acquiring expertise across many industries and technologies, vendors can adapt to changing buyer needs and capitalize on growing opportunities. This may mean making targeted investments in niche capabilities, such as AI solutions for specific sectors, or entering adjacent services arenas, such as digital transformation consultancies.

To effectively manage geopolitical risks, it is crucial for suppliers to communicate frequently and consistently with clients. Suppliers should regularly reach out to clients, understand their concerns, provide information on possible disruptions, and offer a framework of strategies for client-based, technology supply chain risk mitigation. Communication and trust with clients are the foundations of a successful business relationship, especially in uncertain times.

It is essential to have robust practices for assessing and managing risk in place to anticipate and respond to geopolitical challenges. Key practices include continuously monitoring geopolitical developments, scenario planning, and developing contingency strategies. Vendors should also invest in robust data security and business continuity practices to protect client data and ensure the continuity of services.

In sum, the question of how geopolitical forces affect international service outsourcing is complex and multifaceted, with potential risks and opportunities that differ hugely across firms, sectors, and countries. As the industry matures, service outsourcing vendors will necessarily adopt more proactive strategies to identify and mitigate the risks they face. They will become more diversified in their offerings, better in their analytics, and more judicious about which contracts they enter. They will sell knowledge rather than just bodies. They will speak mutter languages. And they will invest instead of play.

CHAPTER 4: EVOLVING BUSINESS MODELS IN OUTSOURCING

The outsourcing business is currently experiencing a fundamental transformation and is heavily influenced by the rapid advancements in artificial intelligence (AI) and also the changing geopolitical landscape. The traditional outsourcing models, which are built on the premise of labor arbitrage and cost reduction, are gradually being replaced by new business models that leverage cutting-edge technologies and focus on value creation. In this chapter, we will analyze the emerging business models in this industry, the pivot of the entire industry to AI-powered solutions, the rise of niche services, and the role of collaboration and partnership.

From labor arbitrage to AI-powered value creation, historically, the driving force behind outsourcing is primarily to cut costs through labor arbitrage by moving relatively low-value activities to counties where labor costs in developing countries are lower. However, with the advent of AI and automation, outsourcing is increasingly centering on technology-enabled value creation. AI-powered models are fundamentally transforming the way services are delivered, enabling vendors to provide efficient, accurate, and scalable solutions.

There is one trend that distinguishes itself, namely that it is hybrid outsourcing models that combine AI capacities with human expertise. These models can help operators of service providers maximize their operations, and keep their costs controlled while improving the quality of service they provide. For starters, an AI-powered bot could handle easy customer inquiries and complaints to provide human agents with more complex, nuanced interactions. The interplay between people and machines is redefining the field of outsourcing and opening new routes for the most creative market leaders.

A different form of market demand is for niche outsourcers. As the industry matures, executive buyers are also interested in specialized services for specific industry verticals or business functions. These 'niche process' examples range from healthcare analytics to financial crime detection to supply chain optimization. Individual companies increasingly want outsourced-for-them solutions to their own, one-of-a-kind problems.

The development of specific AI solutions for industries is the main driver of this trend. By using their domain expertise and advanced analytics, outsourcing vendors can provide custom offerings that address their clients' pain points in a way that's unique to them. For example, a vendor that focuses on healthcare analytics could develop AI-powered tools that help hospitals improve how patients recover, how they allocate resources, and how effectively they avoid readmission.

Another growing opportunity is bespoke AI-driven outsourcing services. In this area, vendors work directly with clients to develop custom AI solutions that are specific to the client's use cases and aligned with their business goals. Vendors that can innovate by working side by side with clients throughout the creation of value will set themselves apart. This is an area where strategic partnerships can be built given the co-creation effort.

In the AI Era, Collaboration and Partnerships Are More Important

As the technology in AI that requires special skills is becoming more complicated, outsourcing companies have formed new alliances and cooperation. The business has started to make strategic partnerships with AI technology providers including computing platforms of the cloud, the establishment of analytics data and research institutions. They want to expand their range of abilities in technology to stay far in front of the capitalization of innovative technology.

By forming these partnerships, vendors can tap into AI tools and platforms at the forefront of technology that can be used to create new services and improve existing ones. For instance, by partnering with a leading cloud computing provider, a vendor can offer its clients scalable, on-demand AI solutions without having to make significant initial investments in infrastructure and talent.

Collaboration in the age of AI is also about co-innovation with customers. By working closely with customers, to understand their specific challenges and business objectives, vendors can build tailored AI solutions that deliver meaningful business results. By working together, this approach creates a feeling of shared ownership and responsibility for the outcome, which in turn improves the results, and solidifies the partnerships.

To wrap up, the outsourcing industry is in the middle of a major transformation right now as old models change and are replaced by new models that are AI-powered and that concentrate on value creation and specialization. The shift towards a hybrid model where some services are outsourced and some are done in-house, the new niche interesting services, and how crucial it is to have a partnership philosophy are all creating lots of new opportunities for vendors and clients.

To excel in this shifting landscape, sellers must foster flexibility, originality, and a customer-first mentality. Employing AI, fostering deep vertical experience, and forging strong partnerships can differentiate sellers in the marketplace and drive game-changing benefits for clients. As the space continues to grow, the innovators and the bold are perfectly primed for what's ahead.

CHAPTER 5: REDEFINING WORKFORCE MANAGEMENT

Artificial intelligence (AI) is increasingly being embraced in the outsourcing industry as firms are recognizing how business models and service delivery can be transformed by broadening AI offerings; and the workforce market reshaped. With AI taking over repetitive and mundane tasks humans have traditionally favored, the role of human talent is shifting. New skills, competencies, and management approaches are required. This article looks at the changing skillset demands in the AI era; it offers insights into what reskilling or upskilling strategies companies might adopt, and it looks at just what exactly a company needs to consider in managing the human-AI interface in outsourcing.

The Changing Skillset Demands in the AI Era As AI continues to permeate the outsourcing arena, the need for technical and analytical skills is growing dramatically. Roles such as data scientists, machine learning engineers, and AI architects are seen as increasingly important to the successful sourcing of AI projects; these professionals are responsible for building, implementing, and managing the AI systems that will power the next generation of outsourcing services.

That said, artificial intelligence is not reducing the importance of domain expertise and industry knowledge. In fact, the combination of technical skills and domain expertise is becoming a crucial differentiator for outsourcing providers. Cross-functional teams, including AI experts, industry specialists, and functional consultants, are becoming increasingly more common in the industry.

Additionally, soft skills such as critical thinking, problem-solving, and creativity are becoming even more valuable in the age of AI. As machines automate routine tasks, human talent will be expected to focus on higher-value activities needing judgment, empathy, and innovation. Outsourcing providers that can develop these skills in their workforce will be well-positioned to provide their clients with value.

Strategies for Reskilling and Upskilling the Workforce To keep up with changing skill requirements, outsourcing providers need to put in place continuous learning and development programs for their workforce. Reskilling initiatives, directed at training employees on new technologies and domains, are critical in ensuring that the workforce remains relevant and competitive.

Upskilling programs, focused on enhancing existing skills and competencies, are equally important. For instance, a customer service representative can be upskilled on usage of AI-powered tools for sentiment analysis and personalized recommendations, to improve the quality of customer interactions.

Another effective approach to workforce development is through partnerships with educational institutions and training providers. Outsourcing providers can work with universities and vocational schools to develop curricula that align with emerging industry trends and skill requirements. These collaborations also give providers a pool of fresh talent with the right mix of domain and technical expertise.

Managing the AI-human interface As AI becomes an integral part of outsourcing operations, managing the AI-human interface becomes a major challenge. Providers have to balance automation and human oversight, deploying the systems in such a way that they work with and augment human abilities.

To effectively manage the human-AI interface, clear communication and transparency are vital. Employees must be told about AI's role in their jobs, the benefits it offers, and how it could affect their roles. Training and support must be provided regularly to help employees integrate AI into their work.

In addition, HR outsourcing providers need to prioritize employee engagement and satisfaction in an AI environment. That may mean rewriting job descriptions to emphasize higher-value tasks, offering ways for workers to grow and learn continuously, and fostering a culture of innovation and collaboration.

Outsourcing providers are navigating a fundamental shift in the workforce landscape as AI is increasingly integrated into business operations and skills requirements change. To survive and thrive in this new environment, providers must build reskilling and upskilling capabilities and forge a new mix of technical and domain-based skills in their workforces. They must also figure out how humans will work, in tandem with AI, in a workplace imbued with Intelligent Automation. Adopting a proactive stance can enable outsourcing providers to better respond to the changes AI is fomenting and, in fact, to use the technology to drive innovation, better service and truly transformative value for their customers. Talent will remain a critical differentiator as the industry evolves in the AI age.

CHAPTER 6: NEW CLIENT RELATIONSHIPS AND DELIVERY

Thanks to AI, outsourcing providers now have a once-in-a-generation chance to change service delivery and the client relationship to the core. By using AI-driven tools and platforms, they can understand the client better than ever before, add value more effectively, and personalize their offerings more comprehensively than we've ever imagined. But getting there is going to require providers to strike the right balance between innovation on the one hand, and trust, transparency, and agility on the other. This chapter will lay out how outsourcing providers can put AI to use in order to improve service desk delivery and client relationships. It's also going to map out the challenges confronting today's sourcing practitioners in this AI era.

AI-Driven and More Personalized Client Insights: AI-driven analytics and machine learning algorithms help outsourcing providers understand their clients' needs, preferences, and behaviors in a more complete way. Providers can mine insight from vast quantities of data from all types of sources, including client interactions, market trends, social media, and so on.

As an example, predictive analytics can help providers anticipate client needs and offer proactive solutions before issues arise. Not only does this demonstrate a deep understanding of the client's business, but it positions the provider as a strategic partner invested in the client's success.

Furthermore, AI can allow outsourcing companies to offer extremely personalized service packages that are custom fit to each customer's specific needs. Employing client information and machine learning algorithms, service providers can change service levels, pricing models, and resource allocation in an adaptive manner to optimize each client's value.

Establishing Trust and Transparency in the AI Epoch Despite AI offering key benefits for client relationships and service delivery, it also introduces new worries around trust and transparency. As AI systems become more complex and autonomous, clients may fret over data privacy, algorithmic bias, and the explainability of AI-driven decisions.

In the AI era, trust is key to outsourcing providers. Trust will come from having transparency and ethical AI as a priority. Being open, honest, and clear to users and clients about the data that is collected and stored is part of transparency. Also providing clients with what AI algorithm is used and how decisions are made to clients to show that you have nothing to hide. Clients want AI transparency in all aspects of AI. Data Security and Privacy are the most important part, you have to make your client's data yours too and show them through your actions that they can trust you to protect it. Data security and privacy are top of the mind with CCPA regulations and the GDPR. The most important thing in trying to build this trust is the transparency that you can offer to your client through these measures.

Additionally, ethical AI frameworks must be developed and complied with by outsourcing providers, and they should focus on fairness, accountability, and transparency. That could include establishing internal governance structures, regularly auditing AI systems and communicating effectively with clients when talking about AI-driven processes.

Agile and Responsive Service Delivery In the fast-paced and dynamic world of AI, agility, and responsiveness are critical to delivering exceptional client service. Outsourcing providers need to adopt Agile methodologies and practices to enable themselves to quickly respond to changes in customers' needs and market conditions.

This may involve adopting iterative development processes, continuous delivery infrastructures, and test automation frameworks to expedite the rollout of AI solutions. By dividing large projects into smaller, more manageable portions, providers can deliver customer value on a more frequent basis and integrate actual feedback. Through AI, vendors may also be able to keep track of their real-time service delivery and proactively detect and fix problems before they adversely affect clients. With AI-powered monitoring and alerts, vendors can assure customers of high service levels, system performance, and security.

Using AI-powered insights and predictions, businesses can make better, more informed decisions about how to allocate resources, what service level to provide, and how to accommodate constantly shifting client expectations – in near real-time. In the era of AI, this ability to be agile and responsive is key to keeping client satisfaction, trust, and loyalty.

AI is changing the way outsourcing providers interact with clients and deliver services. Thanks to AI-powered platforms and tools, providers can more deeply understand client needs, better tailor offerings, and create more value. But to realize these benefits, providers need to follow a strategic model that is anchored by trust, transparency, and agility.

Outsourcing providers who are able to properly leverage AI to enhance customer experience and service delivery, while mitigating the threats posed by the AI era, are the ones who will be most successful moving forward. Service providers that are investing in ethical AI methodologies, robust data security practices, and agile methodologies are making the right investments to create an ongoing, win-win client relationship and drive continual innovation in the world of outsourcing.

CHAPTER 7: AI-ENABLED COMPETITIVE ADVANTAGES

As AI shapes the future of work, innovation is becoming increasingly critical in the outsourcing industry. Outsourcing providers need to build an innovation engine, as more sophisticated and mature forms of AI arrive. By doing so they can stay ahead of the curve and deliver exceptional client value. In this chapter, we'll examine how AI will fuel innovation, the importance of creating sustainable competitive advantage, and the enduring value of an AI-powered outsourcing transformation.

The Role of AI in Driving Innovation AI is a powerful innovation driver in the outsourcing industry. It empowers providers to differentiate their services, simplify their operations, and create unprecedented value for their clients. By deploying AI technologies like machine learning, natural language processing, and predictive analytics, providers can unearth actionable insights, automate complex processes, and devise innovative answers to their clients' most critical challenges.

To begin with, AI has a clear impact within the bounds of new products and services. For example, more and more service providers are developing AI-driven innovation labs or R&D centers. Charged with deploying bleeding-edge technologies and uncovering breakthroughs, these labs consist of multi-compartment squads; a group of data scientists, domain experts, and industry consultants who work together to conceive distinctive solutions that satisfy particular customer demands and market conditions.

To illustrate, a firm that specializes in healthcare services outsourcing might leverage AI to create an enabler that hospitals can use to identify patients who are at high risk for readmission and intervene in order to improve patient outcomes. Likewise, a firm targeting the financial services sector may construct an AI-based fraud detection system that uses machine learning to instantly flag suspicious transactions and halt financial loss.

Creating a last competitive advantage with AI-powered improvement is not enough. Successful outsourcing providers will also need to build their capabilities in ways that are difficult to replicate.

One way to do this is by creating proprietary AI tools and platforms. By investing in developing customized AI solutions for various industries or business processes, providers can differentiate themselves from the competition, and offer clients something they can't get elsewhere. These proprietary tools can be made to integrate with the client's existing infrastructure and operations, which can deliver an unprecedented level of customization and flexibility to clients that generic AI solutions simply can't match.

Another major competitive advantage is talent. Outsourcing providers that can attract, develop, and retain top AI talent will be better positioned to create value and lead their clients through innovation. This necessitates a strong employer brand, competitive compensation packages, and a culture that brings continuous learning and growth to the forefront.

In addition, providers need to build deep domain expertise in the industries they target. By blending AI capacities with industry-specific experience and knowledge, providers can create solutions to address the unique needs and challenges of every sector. Such specialization enables providers to foster long-term partnerships with clients and distinguish themselves from generalist challengers.

Illustrations of AI-Led Outsourcing Transformations that Succeeded To demonstrate how AI-led innovations can transform outsourcing, organizations can review case studies of providers that have transformed their businesses and service portfolios with AI technology.

A case in point is Tata Consultancy Services (TCS), a major IT services and consulting firm. As part of its business process services, TCS has developed a collection of AI-powered tools called TCS Cognitive Business Operations, which applies machine learning, natural language processing, and analytics to reinvent business processes across numerous domains. TCS has deployed these tools with a wide range of customers, yielding substantial cost reductions, operational improvements, and customer experience enhancements.

Wipro is an additional example, this is a global IT, consulting, and business process services company that has taken the next step. They have set up a dedicated AI and automation practice, and they have an end-to-end AI solution portfolio ranging from creation to maintenance. And they have deployed and implemented AI in a wide range of domains, including manufacturing, banking, and healthcare. And they are helping their clients in terms of optimizing their operations, reducing costs, and driving innovation.

These successful AI-driven outsourcing transformations teach us that having a clear AI strategy and strong leadership buy-in is vitally important. A culture of experimentation and continuous learning is also necessary. Providers that can align their AI initiatives with their strategic goals, invest in the right people and technology, and nurture a culture of innovation are likely to succeed in the long term.

AI is completely changing the game in outsourcing, giving providers powerful new ways to drive innovation, differentiate their services, and create client value. By leveraging AI, providers can develop new services and products, build powerful platforms and tools, and enhance domain expertise—and in doing so, create enduring market advantage in a landscape that is increasingly crowded and always in flux.

But AI-driven outsourcing transformations that create value for customers also require more than just technologies. Firms have to establish AI as a core discipline in their organizations and put management systems in place to support it. They must be committed to attracting and retaining top talent in AI by providing competitive compensation packages, establishing strong working relationships with universities, and creating communities where AI researchers and engineers can grow their careers. Just as important, they have to foster a culture of innovation and continuous learning across their organizations. Finally, they need to align their AI initiatives with their overall business goals. By doing so, they can make systematic progress toward their objectives. By learning from the best in the AI business and adopting best practices in AI strategy and implementation, global outsourcing providers can position themselves to reap values from AI in the short term as well as over the long term.

CHAPTER 8: THE ENDURING VALUE OF PEOPLE IN THE AI ERA

In light of the growing adoption of artificial intelligence (AI) and automation in the outsourcing industry, it is vital to acknowledge the timeless worth of human skills and the pivotal contribution humans make to any success of AI-powered initiatives. While AI can automate processes, improve efficiency, and catalyze innovation, it is the human who confers creativity, empathy, and strategic judgment to key equations. This chapter probes the salience of human skills in the AI era, the future of work in outsourcing, and the operation blocks for harnessing a diverse and inclusive outsourcing team.

More than Automation: What Humans Do Best AI and process automation are disrupting the outsourcing industry, but they can't replace the unique skills and talents that humans offer. "Soft skills" such as critical thinking, problem-solving, and creativity are vital in a world of AI-driven outsourcing.

Why? It's these skills that allow outsourcing professionals to approach complex challenges from multiple angles, and then (and here's the important bit) create innovative solutions based on that holistic view. It's these skills that allow outsourcing professionals to react and respond to the market and business shifts that are part and parcel of the world we live in. So, when a client asks for a requirement that's not in the book or your market shifts unexpectedly, what happens next?

Human beings become creative and start creating! Human beings look at the challenge and take a problem-solving approach. Human beings aren't scared of uncertainty, they embrace it and create strategies around it or in spite of it. Basically, human beings respond. They use what they are unique to think differently.

The human element of relationship building, cultural understanding, and client service excellence cannot be automated. Trust, collaboration, and personalized attention to clients require empathy, emotional intelligence, and interpersonal skills that AI cannot replicate.

Outsourcing's Future of Work As AI and automation continue to shape the outsourcing industry, the nature of work and the skills required for success are changing. While some repetitive tasks may be automated, new roles and opportunities are emerging that require a different set of skills and competencies.

In order to be ready for the future of work in outsourcing, suppliers must make workforce transformation investments that revolve around the reskilling and upskilling of their staff. What this looks like in practice is enrolling in various training courses that are geared toward building up both employees' technical skills – particularly, classes in things like data analytics, machine learning, and AI implementation – as well as their soft skills – things like design thinking, storytelling, or change management.

Moreover, outsourcing providers may seek alternative ways as partnering with educational institutions and industry associations, to support these institutions in developing curricula and certification programs that keep up with the rising set of skills required by the industry. By investing in workforce education and development in a proactive manner, these firms can be certain that their teams have the skills and knowledge to prosper in a rapidly changing world of AI. Aside from developing skills, assembling a diverse, inclusive outsourcing team is crucial to success in the world of AI. By pooling people with different viewpoints, backgrounds, and thoughts, diversity offers more imaginative problem-solving, better judgments, and more effective innovation.

In order to attract and keep a diverse workforce, outsourcing suppliers are well advised to develop an encompassing culture that values and allows for differences. This may involve instituting programs for diversity and inclusion training, creating employee resource groups, and ensuring mentorship and sponsorship programs for the underrepresented.

Providers should also take a look at their recruiting and hiring efforts to ensure that they're drawing from a diverse pool and eliminating bias in the decision-making process. By utilizing platforms and tools that are powered by artificial intelligence, providers can help quell unconscious bias and make more quantitative hiring decisions.

Additionally, cultivating an inclusive culture necessitates sustained effort and dedication from leaders. Outsourcing leaders must exemplify inclusive behaviors, articulate the value of diversity and inclusion, and hold themselves and their teams accountable for cultivating an environment that is welcoming and fair.

In a world dominated by AI and automation, the human factor remains a crucial differentiator in outsourcing. By recognizing the lasting primacy of human skills, investing in workforce re-skilling, and structuring diverse and inclusive teams, outsourcing firms can secure and maintain an advantage in the AI-powered world.

As the outsourcing market develops, striking the right balance between AI-based efficiency and human-inspired innovation will be key. Companies that can harness the strengths of humans and machines alike, while establishing a culture that places value on and trusts its people, will outperform in serving clients and drive growth in the age of automation.

CHAPTER 9: FUTURE TRENDS AND RECOMMENDATIONS

As AI rapidly advances and the geopolitical landscape shifts, the outsourcing industry is on the verge of transformation. Outsourcing units need to read the trends as they emerge and adjust their strategies as proactively as possible. In this chapter, we will introduce those emerging AI technologies that will be shaping the new face of outsourcing. Strategic suggestions will be given on both the challenges and opportunities. Last but not least, some final thoughts on the adaptability and flexibility in a global dynamic environment.

AI in Outsourcing's Future: The business of outsourcing is entering a new era with the maturation and extensive applications of AI technologies that are unlocking myriad possibilities for innovation and value creation. The impact is profound and might change the landscape of global outsourcing that we know in the last six decades. Here are six AI trends that change the business foundations or platforms of outsourcing:

1. Cognitive Automation: The integration of artificial intelligence (AI) with robotic process automation (RPA) will give rise to smarter, more flexible automation solutions that require problem judgment and a high level of cognitive functioning.
2. Conversational AI: Advances in natural language processing (NLP) and machine learning will empower chatbots and virtual assistants to operate at a higher level of sophistication, dramatically improving customer services and support functions.
3. AI-powered Analytics: The combination of AI and big data analytics will equip outsourcing providers with visibility into client needs, market trends, and operational performance like

4. Edge AI: By deploying AI capabilities at the edge of networks, closer to your data and your users, a provider can drastically reduce latency, ensure greater security, and cut costs. AI on the edge enables real-time data processing and AI-powered automation on simple devices, without fully relying on the cloud.

In a matter of a few years, the impact of AI has been felt all around the outsourcing industry. Global service providers are in a better place than ever to start innovating and actively applying the technologies in their businesses. The successful use of AI for creating new outsourcing opportunities will depend on whether service providers can orchestrate the technologies effectively and combine them with human processes to be optimal for creating most movies for the buyers and providers in this businesses

Strategic Recommendations for Navigating AI and Geopolitical Challenges: To successfully navigate the challenges and opportunities presented by AI and the shifting geopolitical landscape, outsourcing providers need to consider the following strategic moves:

1. Develop a clear and professional AI Strategy: Outsourcing providers should establish an all-inclusive AI strategy that is in sync with their overall business objectives, identify crucial territories for AI investment and innovation, and outline a roadmap that guides its implementation.
2. Devoting Resources to Cultivate Adequate Talent and Skills: Companies that outsource must dedicate resources to build the requisite talent and skills within their organizations to effectively exploit AI technologies. This might involve the recruitment of AI specialists, re-skilling existing employees, and promoting a culture of persistent learning and innovation.
3. Promote Cooperative Partnerships: Outsourcing providers should look to establish cooperative partnerships with AI technology vendors, educational institutions, and professional

associations to gain access to breakthrough research, exchange best practices, and co-create pioneering solutions.
4. Give Priority to Data Governance and Security: As AI leans heavily on data, providers must safeguard the ethical, responsible use of client data, maintain trust and transparency, and comply with impending data protection regulations.
5. Embrace Agility and Adaptability: With an environment that is constantly changing, providers of outsourcing services must develop agility and adaptability as integral functions. For example, providers should subscribe to agile methodologies, create an experimental culture of continuous improvement, and be well prepared to pivot their strategies in response to new concerns or openings.
6. Broaden the Geographic Reach and Scope of Available Services: Companies interested in outsourcing must diversify their interests geographically and strategically. For example, this may involve looking for areas in which a company is looking to expand, aiming to build expertise in a particular domain, or establishing a network of customers from a variety of sectors and national regions.

We believe outsourcing providers can advance themselves into a position to effectively leverage AI technologies, navigate geopolitical uncertainties, and deliver extraordinary value to their customers by following these strategic recommendations.

Second Wave of Outsourcing Evolution: The outsourcing industry is on the precipice of a new era. The effects of artificial intelligence and the complexities of the geopolitical landscape are creating new markets and new winners. Accelerators of change are creating an imperative to execute a strategy that is agile, adaptive, and decisive; which enables you to keep pace with the competition and prepare to seize tomorrow's advantages. Craft an AI strategy. Invest in upskilling and capabilities development. Practice collaborative partnering. Invest in data governance and security. Champion agility. Broaden your geographic footprint and your services portfolio. These are the seven ways you will succeed in the second wave of outsourcing evolution.

In coming years, global sourcing providers who can expertly harness the power of artificial intelligence (AI) and big data while working harmoniously with humans, navigating complex political, geopolitical, and cross-cultural dynamics with agility and balance, and delivering innovative solutions will survive and grow faster than their peers. The future of outsourcing looks more promising than ever, but success—indeed survival—will require a proactive, strategic, flexible mindset in a global environment that is in constant flux. Challenges are mighty, but opportunities abound for existing players, as well as for newer entrants looking to disrupt the outsourcing landscape with new business models and innovative offerings. To win, excluding the rare case of possessing a market monopoly, global outsourcing providers will have to become a powerful force in shaping the future of business globally and in doing so, effect positive change in the AI era.

ACKNOWLEDGEMENT

In the creation of this seminal series, I have had the distinct privilege of drawing upon the invaluable experiences, insights, and expertise generously shared by a distinguished global network of esteemed partners and accomplished friends. Their direct and indirect contributions have been instrumental, and it is with profound gratitude that I acknowledge the indelible influence they have had on this work.

Kanth Krishnan: Managing Director at Accenture, has been a beacon of inspiration with his incisive insights and visionary leadership in technology services. His profound depth of knowledge and innovative approach have significantly enriched the content of this book.

As Managing Director at Newmark, Jeff Pappas has provided critical perspectives on the dynamic global real estate market landscape. His unparalleled expertise has contributed to a deeper understanding of the business environments explored herein.

Haitao Qi, Chairman of Devott Research and Advisory, has provided exceptionally enlightening perspectives on technology innovations and market trends, especially in the Asian context.

Formerly leading Outsourcing and Managed Services at PwC, Charles Aird's comprehensive knowledge and strategic foresight in outsourcing services have greatly contributed to my understanding of this critical business function.

Mike Beares: Founder and Board Chairman of Clutch.co, has been instrumental in shaping my views on business connectivity through his entrepreneurial spirit and dedication to bridging businesses with the optimal service providers.

It has been my great privilege to learn from and collaborate with these distinguished individuals and institutions operating at the leading edge of our industry. Any merits of this book stem directly from the exceptional global network of friends and partners upon whom I rely. Any faults or shortcomings are solely my own.

Last but not least, the unwavering understanding and support of my beloved wife, Biyu, has been an inspiration to this professional endeavor. The intensive writing workload harkened back to my doctoral dissertation at Yale a quarter-century ago. She remains the driving force behind my career growth and personal fulfillment.

ABOUT THE AUTHOR

Stephan S. Sunn

Stephan Sunn is the Executive Partner at Sanford Black Advisory, a preeminent global business and investment consultancy. In this capacity, he collaborates with industry leaders to advise companies worldwide on growth strategy, marketing/sales, innovation monetization, partnerships, and mergers & acquisitions. Over the past two decades, Mr. Sunn has consulted on sourcing provider selection for more than 30 international corporations and over 20 investment and M&A deals in the technology services, digital technologies, and global outsourcing sectors.

Mr. Sunn possesses particular expertise in empowering private enterprises to accelerate growth and enhance value creation through engagement with governments and technology parks. He holds a leadership position with Devott Co., China's largest private research firm focused on the IT, software, and technology services industries. Additionally, he serves as a Director at the China IT and Outsourcing Association. His clients span Fortune 500 companies, state-owned enterprises, technology parks, SMBs, and startups in both developed and emerging markets.

A graduate of the University of Science and Technology of China (USTC) with a Bachelor of Science degree, and Yale University with a Master of Science and Ph.D., Mr. Sunn frequently shares his insights and research as a speaker at global conferences and events. He is a prolific author and an accomplished presenter for his projects and clients around the world.

BOOKS BY THIS AUTHOR

Competing For The Growth

This book serves as a guidebook for city planners, economic development professionals, tech park builders, and public officials who aim to create thriving innovation communities that attract global trade and stimulate investments. It offers a structured path that begins with intangible factors like vision setting and partnership alignment and extends to pilots and full-blown magnet programs.

The book provides real-life instructions to help put these ideas into practice, including effective strategies for attracting rapidly growing businesses and talent, creating a setting that promotes innovation and entrepreneurship, fostering a competitive and appealing business climate, and building a globally recognized brand and reputation.

The author emphasizes that cities and tech parks must play to their strengths and assets to compete and win in the global arena. The race for relevance is on, and the window of opportunity to determine the outcome is closing. Cities and companies have what they need to succeed, and with the options, relationships, and guidance provided in this book, city managers and tech park authorities can make the decisions necessary to lead their communities to success in the world investment and trade arena.

Searching The New Profits

In the face of global market turbulence and domestic uncertainties, American small and medium-sized businesses (SMBs) and startups have significant growth opportunities in emerging markets. However, these markets also present unique challenges. This handbook provides a semi-analytical and semi-prescriptive approach to help American SMBs and entrepreneurs succeed in these rapidly expanding markets. Conversely, governments, technology parks, and corporations in emerging countries can utilize this book to learn how to collaborate with U.S. companies in their markets to serve their customers effectively.

The book covers essential themes such as researching and identifying matching markets, choosing the appropriate market entry mode, local marketing and sales tactics, effective risk management, establishing an active and reputable presence in the local market, ensuring full legal compliance, avoiding political involvement, talent search and retention, and balancing standardization and localization. The final chapter shares valuable lessons from decades of business practices, acknowledging that readers may have different perspectives on these topics. Expanding knowledge through diverse viewpoints is beneficial for U.S. SMB and startup leaders. Despite the challenges, penetrating foreign markets can be highly profitable, and U.S. enterprises have a reasonable chance of success by capitalizing on the vast potential of these rapidly growing territories.

Cracking The Winning Codes

This book serves as a comprehensive guide for international technology and outsourcing companies seeking to enter and succeed in the highly competitive U.S. market. It emphasizes the importance of adapting to the unique American business culture, which values innovation, diversity, relationships, customer-centricity, and results-oriented management. The guide highlights the need to navigate the complex U.S. regulatory landscape, including federal and state laws, as well as key legislations such as FCPA, SOX, and HIPAA.

The book covers essential topics such as understanding American business culture, complying with legal requirements, developing effective marketing strategies, employing successful sales techniques, addressing cultural differences, and managing risks associated with entering a new market.

Additionally, it encourages the use of innovative tactics to differentiate from competitors and gain market share.

A special section titled "The Lessons" shares the author's personal experiences and insights, providing practical execution tips that focus on solution-oriented approaches, leveraging referrals and testimonials, managing communication costs, delivering higher quality than promised, and investing in proven local sales leaders.

By adhering to the core principles of understanding buyer preferences, continuous innovation, human capital development, risk management, customer-centricity, and resilient operations, global providers can successfully navigate and thrive in the lucrative U.S. market.

Win More Businesses

In the digital age, businesses must navigate the complex landscape of Marketing Technology (Martech) and Sales Technology (Salestech) to stay competitive and drive growth. "Win More Deals in Global Markets" provides a comprehensive guide for leveraging these technologies to enhance customer experiences, streamline processes, and boost revenue across international markets. The book explores the convergence of marketing, sales, and technology, emphasizing the importance of data-driven decision-making and cross-functional collaboration. It offers strategies for overcoming challenges in digital transformation, such as resistance to change and skills gaps, while also addressing the unique considerations of global expansion and localization.

The authors predict future trends in Martech and Salestech, including the increasing role of AI, personalization, and emerging technologies like AR/VR and voice interfaces. Through real-world success stories from global brands like Coca-Cola, Sephora, and Airbnb, readers gain valuable insights into harnessing the power of these technologies for business success. This book serves as an essential resource for executives and professionals seeking to navigate the digital ecosystem and drive growth in the international marketplace.

Renovations Or Revolutions

The book "Renovation or Revolution? Impacts of Latest AI on BPO and Contact-centers Industries" provides an in-depth exploration of the transformative potential of artificial intelligence (AI) within the business process outsourcing (BPO) and contact center industries. It emphasizes the importance of early adoption, customization, and localization of AI solutions to gain a competitive edge in the global marketplace. The book highlights the evolving role of human agents, who will focus on complex problem-solving and relationship-building, while AI handles routine tasks. It also discusses the development of AI expertise within organizations and the ethical considerations surrounding AI implementation.

The authors present a roadmap for incorporating AI, underlining the need for a clear vision, employee training, and continuous improvement. Looking ahead, the book envisions a future of collaborative human-AI partnerships, hyper-personalization, and proactive customer engagement. It stresses that embracing AI is crucial for BPO and contact center companies to achieve sustainable growth and remain competitive in the international arena. The book serves as a comprehensive guide for executives navigating the AI revolution in the global business services industry.

Risky Reefs In The Ocean Of Global Markets

This book provides a comprehensive roadmap for emerging market companies venturing into global expansion. It highlights common pitfalls across strategic planning, finance, operations, human resources, marketing, technology, legal/ethics, and risk management. The book emphasizes thorough market research, cultural adaptation, local partnerships, brand building, innovation investment, and long-term vision.

As the global landscape evolves, it anticipates trends like digitization, sustainability integration, and talent acquisition challenges. The book provides corporate decision-makers with insights and best practices to navigate complexities, mitigate risks, and foster sustainable growth while driving innovation and progress internationally.

The AI Revolution In B2B Marketing And Sales

This professional guidance provides a comprehensive playbook for leveraging artificial intelligence (AI) to drive measurable results in B2B marketing and sales strategies. With insights from real-world case studies spanning diverse industries and business sizes, it explores AI's transformative impact on understanding the AI-empowered buyer, delivering personalized omnichannel experiences, boosting sales productivity, and optimizing operations.

The book offers a strategic framework for successful AI implementation, covering data readiness, talent acquisition, governance, and ethical considerations. Globally applicable principles foster human-AI collaboration, enabling organizations worldwide to harness AI's potential ethically and profitably in the B2B domain.

www.ingramcontent.com/pod-product-compliance
Lightning Source LLC
Chambersburg PA
CBHW072005210526
45479CB00003B/1078